brooches
& pins

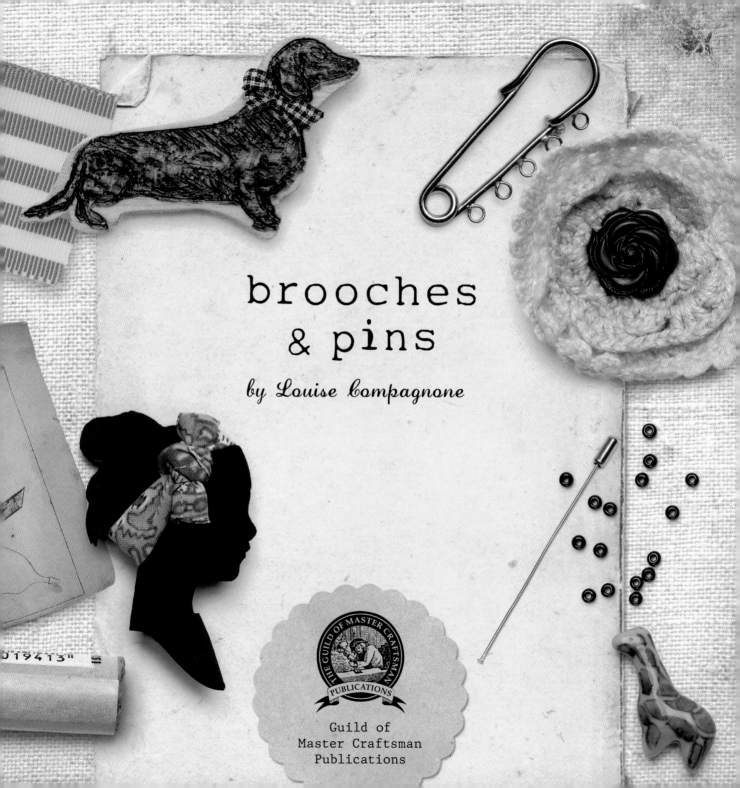

brooches & pins

by Louise Compagnone

Guild of
Master Craftsman
Publications

First published 2011 by
Guild of Master Craftsman Publications Ltd
Castle Place, 166 High Street, Lewes,
East Sussex BN7 1XU

Text © Louise Compagnone, 2011
Copyright in the Work © GMC Publications Ltd, 2011

ISBN 978-1-86108-886-4

A catalogue record for this book is available
from the British Library.

Set in King and Myriad
Colour origination by GMC Reprographics
Printed and bound in China by 1010
Printing Ltd

Publisher Jonathan Bailey
Production Manager Jim Bulley
Managing Editor Gerrie Purcell
Senior Project Editor Wendy McAngus
Editor Simon Smith
Managing Art Editor Gilda Pacitti
Photographers Rebecca Mothersole
and Andrew Perris
Illustrator Anna Compagnone

contents

Tools and materials

Techniques

Continued...

ALICE

ANNIE

LOTTIE

The Projects

FLORA

HENRY

LUCY

CLAUDE

DOTTY

BIRDIE

BETTY

MICKEY

JACQUES

LEE

TATTY

DORIS

JERRY

ALBERT

JAMES

TAVI

DOM

Tools and materials

THIS SECTION DESCRIBES A NUMBER OF DIFFERENT JEWELLERS' TOOLS THAT YOU CAN USE TO MAKE YOUR OWN BROOCHES. I'VE ALSO INCLUDED SOME IDEAS FOR BASIC HOUSEHOLD IMPLEMENTS YOU CAN USE AS THRIFTY SUBSTITUTES.

pliers and scissors

Ideally, it's best to use different types of jewellery pliers for specific projects. But, if you're just starting out, you can get away with using multi pliers for pretty much any job.

ROUND-NOSE PLIERS

Round-nose pliers have smooth, round jaws for making loops and rounded bends in wire.

FLAT-NOSE PLIERS

These pliers have flat jaws for gripping and holding wire and are useful for opening and closing jumprings.

MULTI PLIERS

Multi pliers combine the functions of flat- and round-nosed pliers and wire snips into one handy tool. They are the perfect 'do everything' tool for your brooch projects.

WIRE SNIPS

Wire snips, or snippers, are used for cutting wire and trimming ribbon or leather.

EMBROIDERY SCISSORS

These small scissors have sharp tips for trimming threads closely and accurately.

NAIL SCISSORS

A great substitute if you don't have embroidery scissors, nail scissors have curved blades that also make them great for creating rounded shapes.

ROUND-NOSE

FLAT-NOSE

EMBROIDERY SCISSORS

NAIL SCISSORS

WIRE SNIPS

MULTI

brooch backs and pins

A brooch is defined as any piece of jewellery that can be pinned to clothing. There is a wide range of different findings that you can use to make brooches and pins. The most appropriate one will depend on the materials you are using and the size of your project.

KILT PIN

Traditionally worn on the lower corner of a kilt to prevent it from blowing open, these sturdy pins are also great for making charm brooches. They often have three to five loops, which makes them ideal for attaching beads and charms with jumprings and headpins.

PIN BACK

A pin back, or bar pin, is a hinged pin attached to a long metal finding. Such findings typically have holes so they can easily be stitched or glued to your project.

TALLIS CLIP

Also known as alligator or cardigan clips, tallis clips have flat edges that can be decorated with cabochons, buttons or other embellishments. They are assembled in pairs with a chain.

BUTTON BADGES

These round badges, typically 1in (25mm) in diameter, have a clear plastic cover that you can take off, put the design behind and then place back on top to cover and secure it into place. They come with a metal pin back or a safety-pin-style back.

STICK PIN

Also known as a tie pin, a stick pin is a long, straight pin with a clutch-end safety cover. It can be topped with an ornament and worn vertically on a scarf, tie or lapel.

LAPEL PIN

The lapel, or tac, pin is – as the name suggests – often worn on the lapel of a jacket. It is usually secured with a butterfly clutch that squeezes together to release.

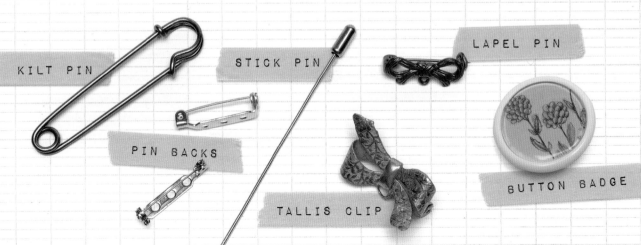

KILT PIN

STICK PIN

LAPEL PIN

PIN BACKS

TALLIS CLIP

BUTTON BADGE

epoxy resin

Epoxy resin is a type of clear plastic made from a two-part solution. It needs to be mixed together before being poured into a mould or bezel setting to set in the required shape. You can set almost any material inside it - from bits of paper to metal charms - giving you endless creative possibilities.

RESIN PIGMENTS AND DYES

Available as liquids, powders or pastes, these can be added during the epoxy-resin-mixing process to give you a wide choice in the colour of your resin brooch. It is important to buy dyes and pigments that are specifically produced for resin and are suitable for the particular brand you're using.

LATEX MOULDS

Because latex is so flexible, these moulds allow you to pop out your resin casting easily. You may need to experiment with your resin mixture, because some brands require some extra hardener to cure in latex.

PLASTIC MOULDS

As with latex moulds, plastic moulds are flexible, making it easy to remove your castings. You can buy moulds specifically designed for resin casting, but they can be expensive, and chocolate moulds or ice trays work just as well.

A bezel or bezel setting is a band of metal with a rim or lip, designed to surround a gemstone. It is also the perfect shape for filling with clear resin and decorative features of your choice such as pretty paper, charms, beads or even cake sprinkles - the possibilities are almost endless.

Tools and materials

textiles

You don't have to be a skilled jeweller to make your own brooches. Forget metal and resin, textiles can create some beautiful results at a fraction of the cost of precious materials.

FELT

Although mainly made from wool, felt is often mixed with fur, cotton, rayon and other materials. Unlike many fabrics that are manufactured by weaving or knitting, felt is formed by working the fibres together using pressure, heat or chemicals. You can buy craft felt sheets in a range of colours, or you can make your own for a more unique look (see pages 24–5 for instructions on how to do this).

LEATHER

Leather is classified according to where it comes from on the animal's body and how it is tanned and treated. Full-grain and top-grain leather comes from the upper layers of the hide and is the highest quality, whereas lower-grade leather, such as split-grain, comes from the innermost parts of the animal. Generally, higher-grade leather is softer and thus easier to sew for your brooch projects. You can often find cheap bundles of leather scraps in fabric and craft stores.

GROSGRAIN RIBBON

Rather than being smooth to the touch, the fibres of this ribbon are woven so you can see and feel the line of weave. It comes in all colours and designs, and is ideal for using to create strong borders for your projects.

RIC RAC RIBBON

Ric rac is ribbon that has been cut or woven in a zigzag shape. First popular in the 1970s, it has since made a comeback with the latest revival of cool retro crafts. Available in a range of different textures and colours, it can add a fun twist to your brooches.

SATIN RIBBON

Usually made from fabrics such as nylon or polyester, this ribbon has a glossy surface and comes in a variety of weaves, including plain and twill.

VELVET RIBBON

Great for adding a tactile quality to your projects, this soft ribbon is textured on one side and flatter and smoother on the reverse side.

SILK RIBBON

Ribbon made from 100 per cent silk is lightweight and has a sleek feel to it. Its luxurious finish can evoke a sense of vintage elegance.

SILK CORD

Made from several strands of silk woven, braided or twisted together, silk cord comes in a variety of thicknesses. Thin cord is ideal for beading, and thicker cord is great for borders and nautical knots.

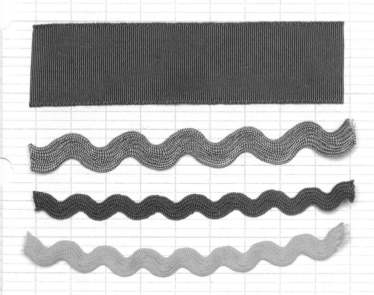

Tools and materials

thread

When buying thread for your projects, try to choose
a shade darker than your fabric so that it blends in
harmoniously. If the fabric is patterned or multicoloured,
select a thread that corresponds to the most dominant colour.

COTTON AND COTTON-POLYESTER

This is the thread of choice for crafters because it is strong,
durable, doesn't stretch and is easy to use. You will often
see it described as 'mercerized', meaning that it has been
repeatedly processed to give added lustre to its surface.

SILK

Not only does this thread have a gorgeous sheen, it is
the most trouble-free to use. It is strong, durable and,
like cotton-polyester, doesn't stretch.

WOOL AND ACRYLIC

Often used for embellishments, wool and acrylic threads
are heavy, fuzzy threads that require a large-eyed needle.

EMBROIDERY

Embroidery thread, or floss, is formed from a number of
strands twisted together, often made from Egyptian cotton.
Its thick width makes it perfect for securing embellishments
and sewing contrast borders.

INVISIBLE

Almost invisible, this thin nylon thread is popular because
it is forgiving of flawed stitching and cannot be easily
detected. It is sold either clear
or with a smoky hue for using
with darker fabrics.

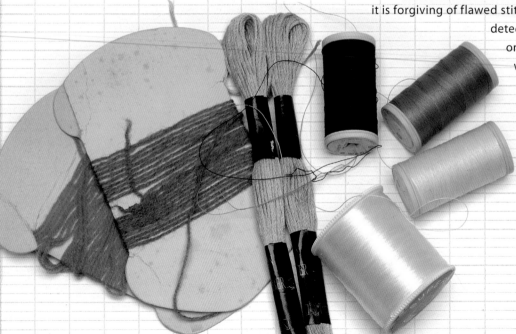

needles

Hand-sewing needles vary in thickness, point shape, length and the size of the eye, depending on the task, technique, type of thread or yarn they are designed to be used with. To get the best results in your projects, use a needle that is small enough to stitch through the fabric without stretching it, but strong enough not to break or bend.

BEADING NEEDLES

(Sizes 10–15) These are long, thin needles used for sewing beads and sequins onto fabric.

EMBROIDERY NEEDLES

(Sizes 1–10) These needles are the same length and point as an ordinary sharp needle but with an elongated eye for threading embroidery floss.

GLOVERS' NEEDLES

(Sizes 3–10) These needles feature a triangular point and will pass through thicker materials such as leather, suede, vinyl and plastic without tearing them.

SHARPS NEEDLES

(Sizes 1–12) Medium length with a round eye and sharp point, these standard sewing needles can be used for a multitude of hand-sewing projects.

TAPESTRY NEEDLES

(Sizes 13–28) With a large eye (so you can thread yarn or several strands of floss or thread) and a blunt end, these needles are ideal for undertaking embroidery and decorative stitching on loosely woven fabrics without damaging the cloth.

NEEDLE THREADER

A needle threader consists of a handle and a wire hoop. To use it, place the hoop through the eye of your needle, push your thread through the wire and then pull the wire back through the eye, bringing the thread with it.

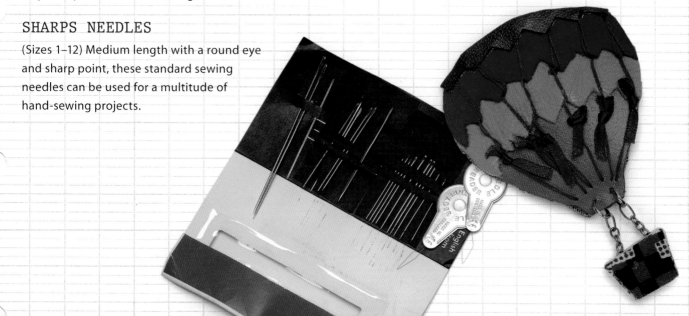

Tools and materials

Techniques

THE BROOCH PROJECTS IN THIS BOOK USE A VARIETY
OF TECHNIQUES - FROM CASTING AND WOOD BURNING TO SEWING
AND KNITTING. ALL OF THEM ARE EASY, USE INEXPENSIVE
TOOLS AND ARE SUITABLE FOR BEGINNERS.

casting with epoxy resin

Epoxy resin is a type of plastic that you can manipulate in
its liquid state and pour into moulds to make a shape of your
choice. When using resin, make sure you wear gloves, cover
your work surfaces and keep the room well-ventilated.

BEFORE CASTING, MAKE SURE
YOUR MOULDS ARE DUST FREE
AND SPRAY THEM LIGHTLY WITH
COOKING OIL. THIS WILL MAKE IT EASIER
TO REMOVE YOUR RESIN CASTING LATER.

Brooch pins

USING EPOXY RESIN

1 Use disposable plastic cups to mix and measure two parts resin to one part hardener. Pour resin into the first cup. Mark the level before pouring it into a second cup.

2 Add hardener to the first cup up to the marked line then pour it into the second cup containing the resin.

3 Stir for two minutes with a stick, constantly scraping the sides as you mix.

4 Now pour the resin into the moulds along with any decorations you are using.

5 Cover the moulds to prevent dust from settling and leave to set for 24 hours.

6 Check that the resin is no longer sticky to the touch. If so, the castings are ready to remove; if not, leave for a further 24 hours.

7 To remove, turn the moulds upside down and lightly tap the back of each piece.

8 Finally, turn them the right way up and push your castings out of each mould.

Techniques

sewing

These basic hand-sewing techniques will help you finish your brooch projects with flair. If you're new to sewing - or just very short sighted like me - don't worry if your stitches are a bit uneven. Imperfection can add a certain charm (well that's what I tell myself anyway).

RUNNING STITCH

Running stitch is the simplest hand-stitch, and it can also be used to create lovely decorative edges on your projects. For the neatest results, try to make all of your stitches the same length.

1 Thread your needle and knot the tail end.

2 Pull the needle and thread through the back of your fabric.

3 Now pass the needle in and out of your fabric at even intervals.

4 Repeat until you reach the required number of stitches.

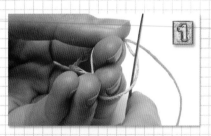

SEWING LEATHER

As leather is so dense it is very difficult to sew it using an ordinary needle. It is best to use a special leather needle - which has a chiselled head and very sharp point - combined with a thick, waxed thread. When pushing the needle through, be sure to protect your fingers by using a thick thimble.

BACKSTITCH

Backstitch creates a neat run of stitches to reinforce your projects, as well as giving them an attractive finish. It's similar to a basic sewing machine stitch, without all the carry on!

1 Thread your needle and knot the tail end. Make one running stitch. Push the needle up through the fabric one space to the right.

2 Finish the stitch by pushing the needle back into the fabric at the point it was first pulled through, and push to the back.

3 Push the needle up through the fabric one space to the right to make further stitches.

 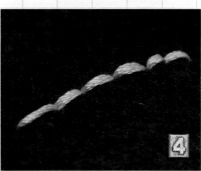

4 Repeat this process until you have the required number of stitches.

BLANKET STITCH

Blanket stitch can be used to reinforce the edges of thick fabrics, and is traditionally used for this purpose to make blankets. This versatile stitch is also a perfect way to join together two layers of fabric and can add a lovely, decorative border to plain materials.

1 Thread your needle and knot the tail end. Start between the two layers and poke your needle down through the bottom layer. This will keep your knot hidden.

2 Start to make a running stitch to the right. Rather than pulling your needle all the way through, create a loose loop.

3 To anchor your stitch, pull it through the loose loop.

4 Make a running stitch to the right.

5 Repeat the process from step 3 onwards, keeping the steps as even as possible.

6 Continue until you reach the required number of stitches.

pyrography

Pyrography is the ancient art of decorating wood or leather by burning designs onto the surface with a heated tool. Traditionally pokers or other hot irons were used, but today specialist wood-burning pens are available with all sizes and shapes of nib - although you can also use a heated soldering iron as a thrifty substitute.

USING A WOOD-BURNING TOOL

It's a good idea to practise handling the tool with the power off so that you get a feel for it. You should hold it like a pencil, but only on the protected part. Once you feel happy with your chosen implement, try it out for real on a piece of scrap wood.

1 Switch on your iron and allow it to heat up.

2 While you're waiting for your tool to heat up, draw your design onto the wood in pencil.

3 Use your tool to trace around the outlines of your design, then rub out the pencil marks.

4 After this you can fill in dark areas and shading. You can create different shades by varying your drawing speed. Working slowly means the wire touches the wood for longer so makes a darker line; working faster creates a lighter shade.

5 Once you're satisfied with the result, apply a coat of varnish to give your artwork a professional finish.

knitting

Once you master basic knitting stitch, the trickier stitches will follow on naturally. Soon enough you'll be ready to invent your own knitted brooch projects.

CASTING ON

There are various methods of starting a knitting project, known as casting on. You can either use one needle along with your thumb or two needles. My mother taught me to cast on with two needles, so this is the method I'll explain to you. It creates the firmest, neatest finish.

1 Make a slipknot by winding the yarn around two fingers then over again to the back of the first thread.

2 Use a knitting needle to pull the back thread through the front one, forming a loop.

3 Pull the end to tighten the loop.

4 Place the slipknot onto your left needle and tighten it.

5 Insert your right needle through the slipknot and wrap the wool over your right needle.

6 Draw the yarn through the first loop to create a new one.

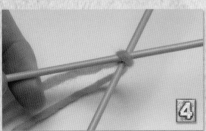
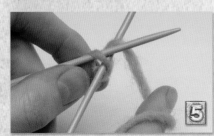

BASIC KNITTING

There are many different types of knitting stitch, each creating a different visual effect. The most popular are plain knit, pearl, stocking, yarn over and knit two together. I'm going to explain how to do the most basic stitch: plain knit.

1 Starting with the yarn at the back, insert your right needle in through the front of the first stitch on your left needle.

2 Wind the yarn around your right needle.

3 Pull the loop through.

4 Slip the original stitch off your left needle.

5 Repeat until all the stitches have been transferred from the left to your right needle. Swap sides and continue.

7 Slide the new stitch onto your left needle. Insert the right needle into the new stitch and repeat steps 5–6 to make another new stitch.

8 Repeat until you have enough stitches for your project.

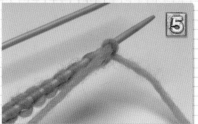

felting

Using ready-made felt squares is a bit like painting with colours
straight from the tube - it's easy but not always very interesting.
If, however, you're patient enough to make your own felt,
you can get some beautiful and unique results.

Felting is caused
by heat and friction, so
choose the settings on your
washing machine that use
the least water, the highest
temperature and most
agitation possible.

MAKE SURE YOU CAREFULLY WEAVE IN THE

ENDS OF YOUR KNITTED SQUARES BEFORE

PUTTING THEM IN THE WASHING MACHINE.

OTHERWISE THEY COULD WORK LOOSE WHILE

THEY ARE FELTING AND CAUSE A HOLE

IN YOUR YOUR WORK.

CREATING FELT

1 Start by knitting squares in the colours you want to use for your project. Most brooches you make shouldn't require squares bigger than 25 stitches.

2 Place your squares into an old pillowcase so that they don't get lost inside the machine. You can add some cotton items to the machine to increase the friction.

3 If you have a top-loading machine, set it to a ten-minute hot cycle and check; continue for an additional ten minutes if you're not satisfied with the results. If you have a front loader, knit a few extra squares so that you can try a number of different cycles and compare the results.

4 As your knitting goes through the felting process, the stitches will become smaller and eventually disappear. The squares will also gradually get smaller. Different wools will give different results – some shrink more than others – so you need to experiment to see which suits your purposes best.

5 Once the knitted stitches have disappeared and your fabric feels firm and thick, the process is complete. Don't be tempted to continue because the fabric will become unworkable.

using jumprings

Jumprings are simple loops of wire that you can use to connect bits of jewellery together. If you are planning on using them in a number of projects, it's cheap and easy to make your own. But as I'm using them only in a couple of brooch projects, I've decided to use the ready-made version.

OPENING AND CLOSING JUMPRINGS

It is important to know how to open and close jumprings without causing them to lose their shape.

1 Take two pairs of pliers, one in each hand (flat-nose, bent-nose and chain-nose pliers all work well).

2 Clasp either side of the jumpring so the split is in the centre.

3 To open the ring, move one hand away from you gently while you move the other towards you.

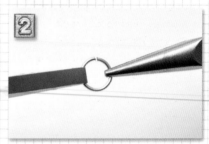

To close the ring, reverse the technique by moving one hand towards the other until the two ends are flush against one another again.

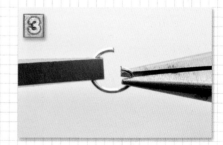

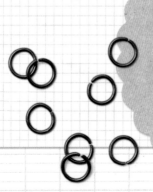

DON'T OPEN YOUR JUMPRING BY PRYING THE ENDS APART SIDEWAYS. THIS WILL WEAKEN THE METAL AND WARP ITS SHAPE.

using eyepins

Eyepins are small pins with a tiny loop at one end, used for joining one jewellery component to another. They are similar to jumprings, only with a length of wire for placing beads and other ornamental items onto.

THREADING AN EYEPIN

1 Thread beads onto the eyepin.

2 Use round-nose pliers to bend the wire about 90 degrees.

3 Use a wire cutter to cut off excess wire, leaving about $^3/_{16}$ in (5mm) to play with. Carefully bend this piece of excess wire into a loop using round-nose pliers – but don't close it all the way.

4 Attach the loop to your other jewellery finding and close it gently.

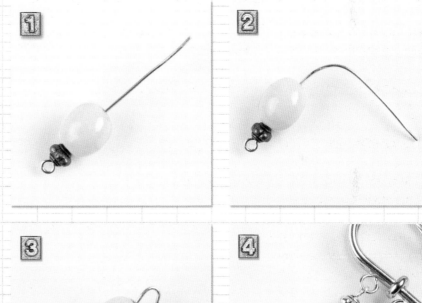

ceramics
and resin

alice

It's always time for a
drop of tea when you're
wearing the party!

Everything you will need...

Dolls' house accessories such as teapots and cups make gorgeous charms to hang from kilt pins. You can find dolls' house miniatures in most craft stores and online stores (see Resources on page 118).

1 Dolls' house ceramic teapot and 4 x matching cups

2 5 x silver jumprings

3 Silver kilt pin with five loops

4 Artists' dry pastel in beige

Clear epoxy resin

Disposable plastic cups

Stirring stick

Round-nose or flat-nose pliers

AUTUMN BROWN • MARRON D' AUTOMNE

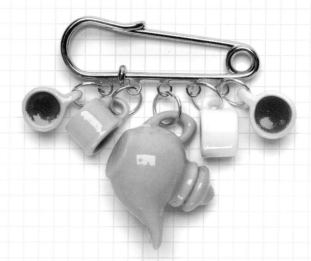

Assembling alice

1 Mix together the clear epoxy-resin solution in a disposable plastic cup (see instructions on pages 16–17).

2 Rub the inside of another plastic cup with the dry pastel until you have about a teaspoon of chalky powder.

3 Transfer the resin solution to the cup containing the pastel powder and stir until dissolved.

4 Pour the resin solution into each of the miniature ceramic cups. Cover and leave to dry for 24 hours.

5 Attach the handle of the teapot to the middle loop of the kilt pin using a jumpring.

6 Finally, using jump rings, attach all four mugs – containing their resin 'tea' – to the kilt pin, one on each loop.

WHEN WORKING

WITH RESIN, ALWAYS

WEAR GLOVES TO

PROTECT YOUR HANDS.

annie

This casting project
is so deliciously simple
you'll want to eat it.

Everything you will need...

Just mix together some resin solution, pour it into a mould along with a pinch of cake sprinkles and let the magic happen.

1 Cake sprinkles

2 Heart-shaped rubber mould (approximately 8½ x 4½in (215 x 115mm)

3 1in (25mm) pin back

Clear epoxy resin

Disposable plastic cups

Stirring stick

Craft glue

Assembling annie

1 Line your mould with a light spray of cooking oil and mix together the clear epoxy-resin solution in a disposable plastic cup (see instructions on pages 16–17).

2 Pour a small amount of the resin solution into your mould, followed by a thimbleful of sprinkles, then more resin until the mould is half full. Cover and leave to set for 12–24 hours.

3 Turn your mould over and tap gently on the back.

4 Turn it over again and push the back firmly until your resin heart pops out.

5 Wipe off any remaining oil.

6 Turn your resin heart over and glue a pin back to the back.

IF CAKE SPRINKLES DON'T GET YOUR MOUTH WATERING YOU CAN REPLACE THEM WITH ANY TINY COLOURFUL MORSELS.

annie

lottie

These cute giraffe beads, which
I bought from a market in Vietnam,
make a perfect charm pin.

Everything you will need...

If you can't find your own tall spotty creatures, any brightly coloured ceramic beads will do (see Resources on page 118 for some excellent online jewellery stores).

1 5 x silver eyepins

2 2 x ceramic animal beads

3 5 x ceramic barrel beads

4 12 x metal spacer beads

5 Silver kilt pin with five loops

Round-nose pliers

Wire cutters

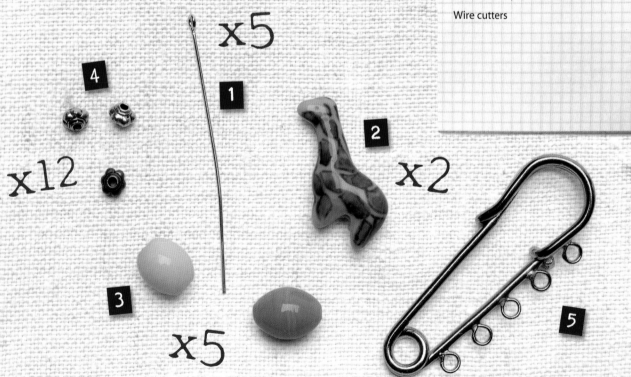

x5

x12

x2

x5

lottie

Assembling lottie

1 Thread a metal spacer, a ceramic barrel bead followed by another metal spacer onto an eyepin.

2 Use your pliers to bend the end of the eyepin 90 degrees.

3 Trim off all but ³/₈in (10mm) from the end of the eyepin using your wire cutters. Curve the ³/₈in (10mm) end with your round-nose pliers, leaving the loop slightly open.

4 Attach the wire pin to the first loop of the kilt pin, before closing it using your pliers.

5 Repeat steps 1–3 to make two more eyepins with barrel beads and attach them to the third and fifth loops of the kilt pin.

6 Thread two eyepins with a metal spacer either side of a ceramic animal bead, followed by a ceramic barrel bead and another metal spacer.

7 Repeat steps 1–2 on your two animal-bead eyepins.

8 Finally, attach the two sets with animal-beads to the remaining loops on the kilt pin.

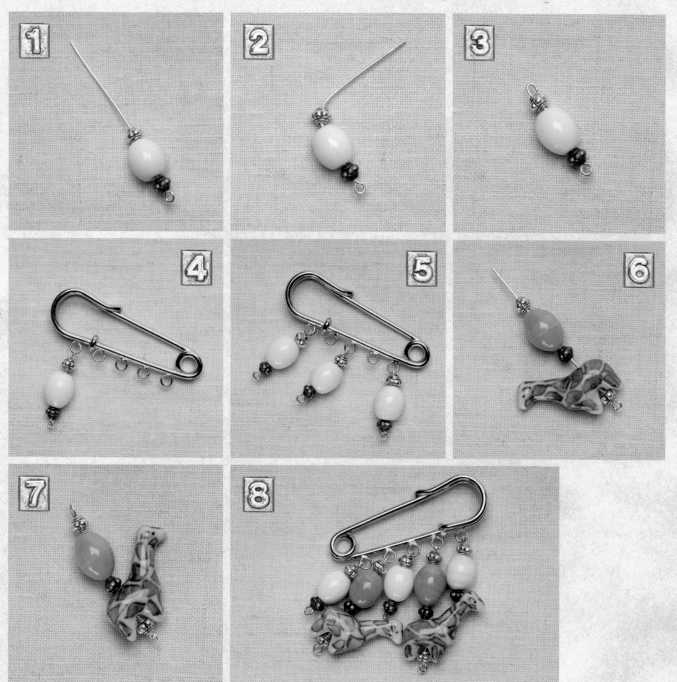

flora

Some pictures are too
lovely to hide away
inside a locket.

Everything you will need...

To make this charming floral
decoration, just add pretty paper
or a page from an antique book
and hang from a tie-pin finding.

1. Brass locket with space
   on the front for a picture
2. Pretty paper or a page
   from an antique book
3. Brass tie pin with loop
4. Jumpring
   Round-nose or flat-nose pliers
   Clear epoxy resin
   Disposable plastic cups
   Stirring stick
   Nail scissors

flora

Assembling flora

1 Place your locket underneath the paper and trace around the inside ridge of the locket 'picture frame' using a pencil.

2 Trim around the edge of the pencil outline using nail scissors, leaving the paper shape to be framed.

3 Put your paper shape inside the locket picture frame in order to check whether it fits. Trim the paper if necessary.

4 Mix together the clear epoxy resin solution in a disposable plastic cup (see instructions on pages 16–17).

5 Pour the resin into your locket over the paper shape until it is completely covered, being careful that it doesn't spill over the edge of the frame. Leave to set for 24 hours.

6 Attach the locket to the loop of the tie pin using a jumpring.

wood and
paint

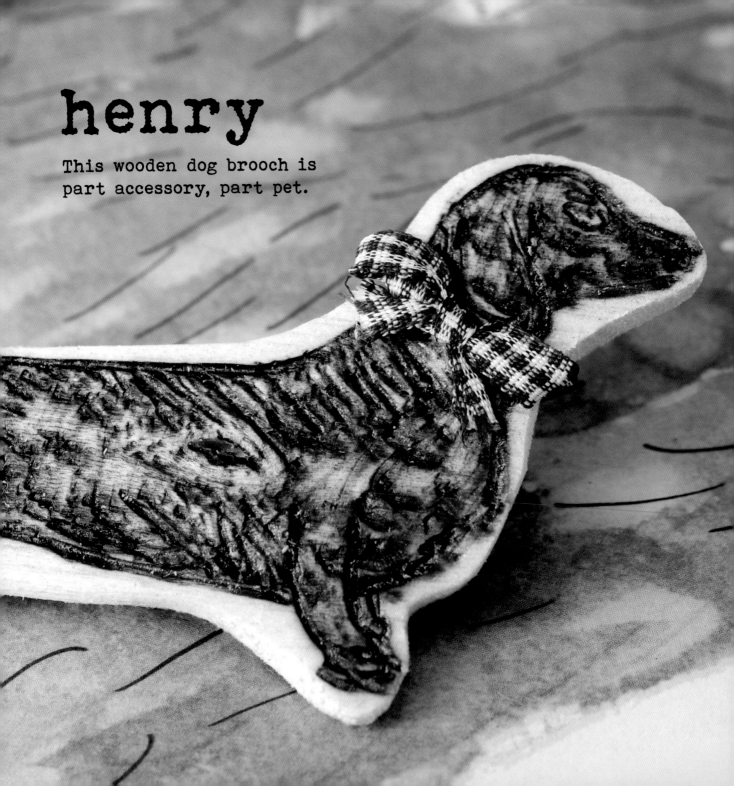

henry

This wooden dog brooch is
part accessory, part pet.

Everything you will need...

With a steady hand and a little bit of imagination, you can create eye-catching wooden brooches using a pyrography tool. Pin this doggie to a pretty blouse and enjoy his handsome face looking back up at you.

1. Small piece of balsa wood, around 4½ x 2½in (115 x 65mm)
2. Photocopy of dog design
3. Small piece of thin, patterned ribbon
4. 1in (25mm) pin back

Pyrography tool or soldering iron

Fine sandpaper

Scalpel

Craft glue

Ballpoint pen

1

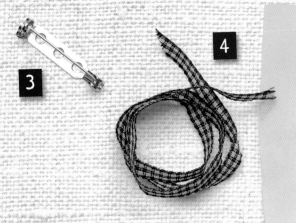

3

4

2

henry

Assembling henry

1 Cut around the photocopied dog design, leaving at least a ½in (13mm) border. Place the dog design onto the balsa wood and trace around the main lines using a ballpoint pen, pressing down firmly.

2 You will be left with a dog-shaped imprint on the balsa wood.

3 Trace the lines of the dog imprint with your pyrography tool or hot soldering iron as neatly as possible (see instructions on page 21).

4 Now use your tool to add detail to the body of your dog, roughly following the photocopied design.

5 Cut around the dog outline using a scalpel.

6 Leave a ¼in (6mm) border around your design.

7 Smooth the rough edges with sandpaper.

8 Using the ribbon, make a tiny bow the same width as your dog's neck. Attach the ribbon to the neck with a dot of craft glue.

9 Finally, glue the pin back to the back of your dog, making sure it is centred.

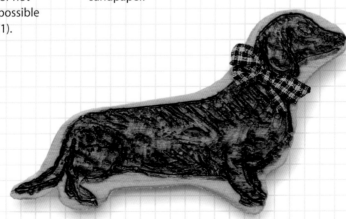

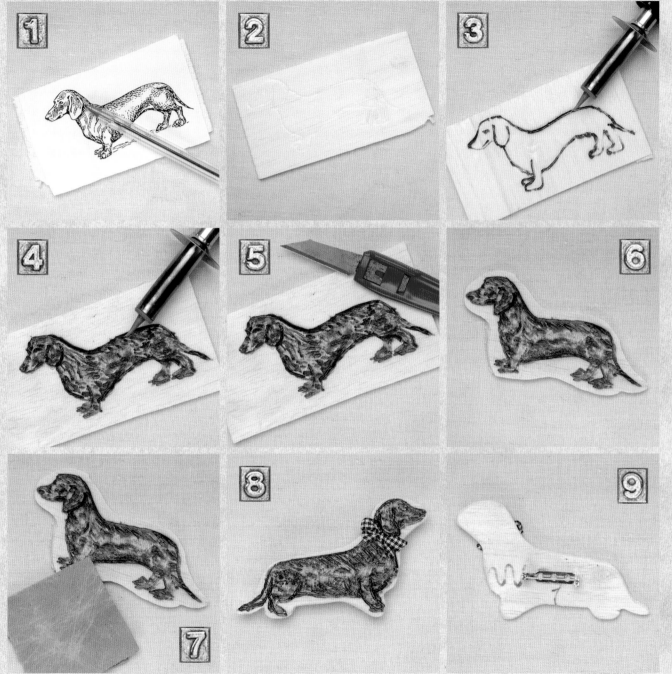

lucy

This quirky telephone brooch is sure to be a conversation piece!

Everything you will need...

Use transfer glaze to transfer any printed or photocopied image to your wooden brooch projects for a professional result that says, 'Hello, I'm fabulous.'

1 Small piece of balsa wood, larger than your image

2 Photocopy of telephone design

3 Scrap of thin cord

4 1in (25mm) pin back

Transfer glaze

Sponge applicator or paintbrush

Craft glue

Scalpel

Sandpaper

Scissors

Assembling lucy

1 Trim around the edge of the photocopied telephone design.

2 Paint two layers of transfer glaze – horizontally – onto the face of the design, leaving 20 minutes between coats. Then paint two further layers of transfer glaze – vertically – onto the face of the design, again leaving 20 minutes between coats. Set aside for two hours to cure.

3 Place your design face down in a bowl of warm water. Leave for 20 minutes.

4 Remove from the water and place face down onto a hard, smooth surface. Gently rub the back of the transfer with your fingertips until the paper starts to peel off. Keep doing this until all the paper has been removed leaving the image on the transfer glaze. Cut around the very edge of your transfer design to remove any excess.

5 Paint a coat of transfer glaze onto one side of the balsa wood.

6 Position the transfer on the wood and rub with your fingertips to smooth and remove any air bubbles. Allow to dry, then apply another coat of transfer glaze on top of the transfer. Allow to dry once again.

7 Cut into the balsa wood with a scalpel, following the outline of your telephone. Smooth off any rough edges with sandpaper.

8 Glue both ends of the cord to the back of your telephone.

9 Finally, glue on the pin back so it is perfectly centred.

SPEED UP THE WAITING TIME BETWEEN APPLYING COATS OF TRANSFER GLAZE BY USING YOUR HAIRDRYER.

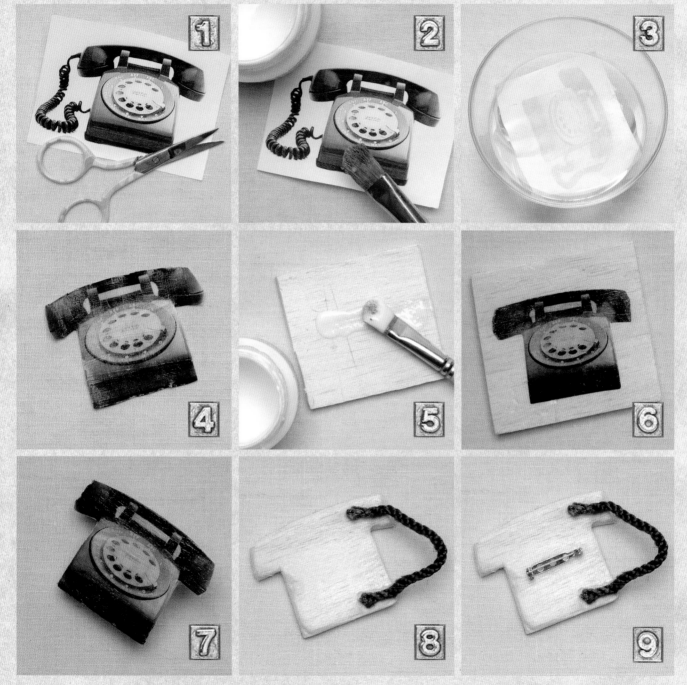

claude

This darling miniature artist's palette will make your outfit zing like a Monet original.

Everything you will need...

Simply mix some pretty colours from acrylic paint, dab them onto your palette, apply a glaze and you have yourself a charming accessory.

1 Small piece of balsa wood, around 4 x 4in (100 x 100mm)

2 A selection of acrylic paints

3 Wooden skewer cut down to 1in (25mm) in length

4 1in (25mm) pin back

5 Two small paintbrushes

Varnish for acrylic paint or clear nail varnish

Craft glue

Fine sandpaper or emery board

Nail scissors

x2

IF YOU FIND IT HARD TO CHOOSE
A COLOUR PALETTE FOR YOUR PROJECTS,
TAKE INSPIRATION FROM VINTAGE FABRICS.

Assembling claude

1 Draw a palette shape onto the balsa wood and cut out using nail scissors. Sand all edges smooth using fine sandpaper or an emery board.

2 To make the thumb hole, poke out a small hole using the tip of a pen, then gently enlarge it using the end of your paintbrush.

3 Mix acrylic paint to make a range of different colours – don't just use tones straight from the tube, but try to create your own unique palette. Place a small blob of each colour around the edge of the palette and allow to dry thoroughly before applying a thin coat of varnish.

4 To make a tiny brush handle, paint the wooden skewer in a colour of your choice and allow to dry. Pull the metal end off a small paintbrush, squeeze some glue inside and then push it onto the end of the skewer to complete your miniature paintbrush.

5 Finally, glue your paintbrush to the palette and leave to dry before gluing the pin back to the back.

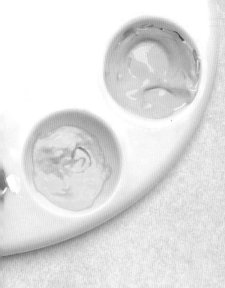

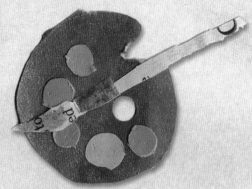

WHEN CUTTING BALSA
WOOD, ONLY CUT A
SMALL SECTION AT
A TIME TO PREVENT
IT FROM SPLITTING.

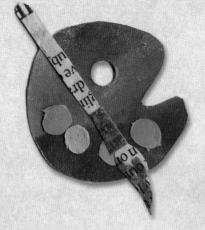

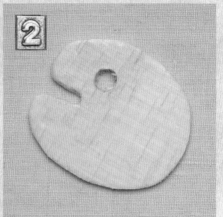

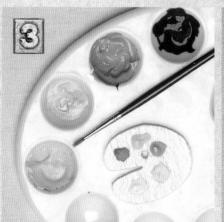

claude

dotty

My mum made a brooch
like this for me when
I was a child, and I've
loved it ever since.

Everything you will need...

Unlike me, who drops more stitches than I 'catch', my mother has always been an incredible knitter. But if I can make this, so can you!

1 Wool oddments

2 2 x wooden skewers

3 Kilt pin with five loops

4 5 x jumprings of the same metal as the kilt pin

Thin knitting needles, around 2–4mm

2 x wooden beads that will fit on the end of the skewers

Craft glue

x5

Assembling dotty

1 Cut a 1½in (40mm) length from both wooden skewers at the pointed end. Add a blob of glue to the blunt end and top with the wooden beads.

2 Cast on eight stitches using your thin knitting needles then knit five rows of plain knit (see instructions on casting on and plain knitting on pages 22–3).

3 Gently pull your knitting off your needles and slide onto one of the skewers, being careful not to catch the wool with the pointed end.

4 Take your other skewer and insert it into your knitting at a 45-degree angle so that the points of the two skewers almost meet.

5 Roll a small ball of wool – about ½in (13mm) wide – in the same wool as your knitting, leaving a loose strand.

6 Attach the wool ball to your knitting by knotting it to the loose strand.

7 Trim off the loose strand and glue the ball to the bottom left-hand corner of your knitting.

8 Finally, join your knitting to the kilt pin using jumprings (see instructions on opening and closing jumprings on page 26), looping them through the stitches you cast on in step 2.

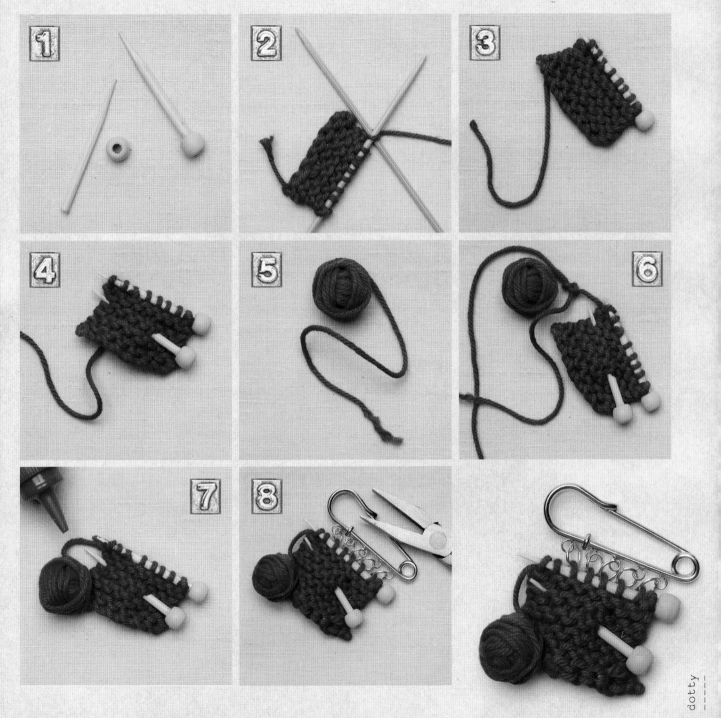

felt and
leather

birdie

Hello birdie, bye-bye
time-consuming projects.

Everything you will need...

Using scraps of fabric and felt, you can create simple 'feathers' for your little sparrow brooch.

1. Off-cuts of felt in magenta, yellow and brown
2. Floral fabric scraps
3. Cream cotton thread
4. 1 x black seed bead
5. 1in (25mm) pin back
Scissors
Needle
Craft glue

birdie

Assembling birdie

1 Cut out felt and fabric shapes using the templates below.

2 Glue larger 'feather' shapes onto the bird silhouette so they fan out, lifting up the right-hand ends slightly to allow the smaller shapes to slide underneath.

3 Glue three of the small feather shapes under the large shapes so that only the end peeks out. Glue the final small feather shape on top of the previous layers.

4 Sew the black seed bead into place to form the bird's eye and sew around the edges with running stitch using cream cotton thread.

5 Secure a pin back into place on the reverse side by threading it through a small felt square and gluing the square into place.

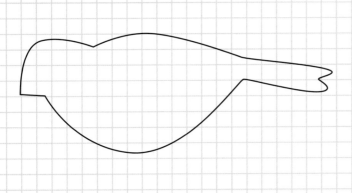

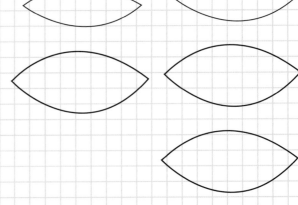

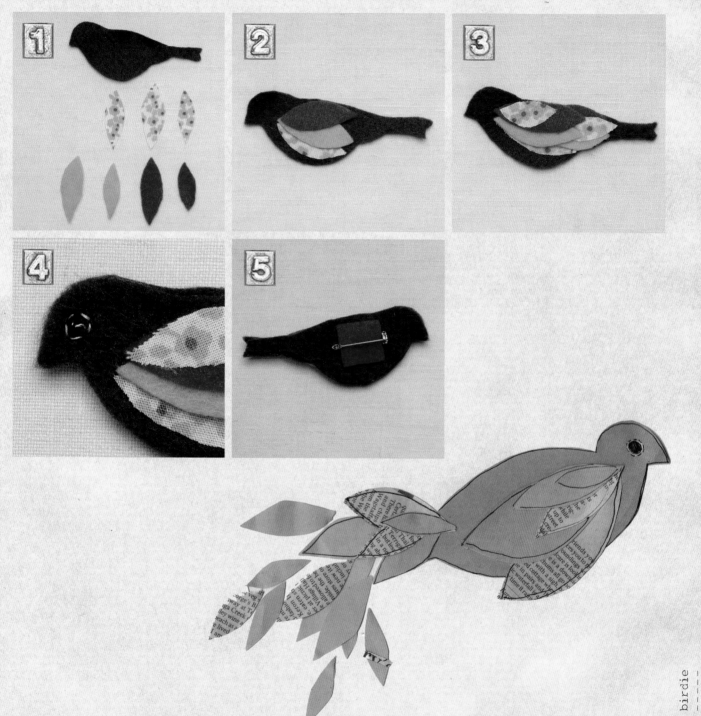

betty

Bring out the sunshine
with a colourful felt
apple brooch.

Everything you will need...

This project is as easy as apple pie to make – just stitch, glue, pin and go.

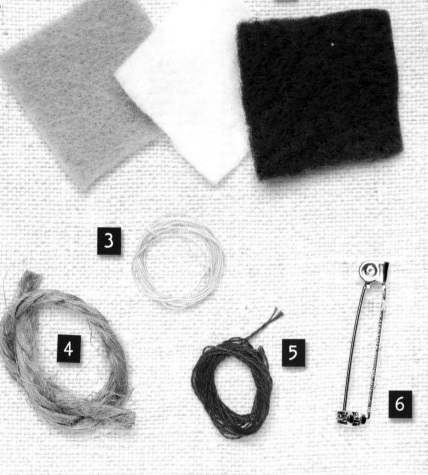

x8

1 Felt squares in red, green and white

2 8 x black seed beads

3 Beige cotton thread

4 Kitchen string

5 Red cotton thread

6 1in (25mm) pin back

Scissors

Needle

Assembling betty

1 Using the templates cut out two large red and two small white apple shapes from the red and white felt squares.

2 Place the two white apple pieces on top of one another and sew together around the border with blanket stitch (see instructions on page 20) using the beige thread.

3 Group two lots of four seed beads in the middle of the white apple shape and secure, either by sewing or gluing. Now sew an oval around them, then a line from the oval to the top and to the bottom in running stitch.

4 Place the red apple pieces on top of one another and sew around the edges with blanket stitch using the red cotton thread.

5 Glue the white felt pieces onto the red felt pieces and leave to dry.

6 Cut out a leaf-shaped piece from the green felt square using the template and sew along the centre in running stitch using beige thread.

7 Place the leaf on top of the apple along with a 1in (25mm) length of string to form a stalk. Glue or sew the leaf and stalk into place.

8 Secure a pin back to the back either by gluing or sewing.

GLUING THE VARIOUS ELEMENTS OF THE DESIGN TOGETHER IS QUICKER AND EASIER BUT SEWING THEM CREATES A NEATER, MORE SECURE FINISH.

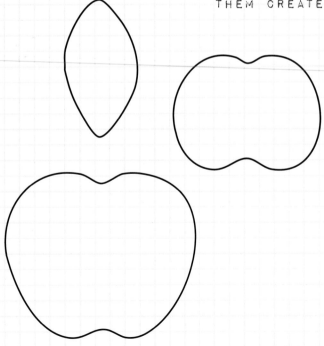

mickey

Pin it to your beret, headband or
right in the centre of your collar.
Not only is this tiny leather bow
tie versatile, it is guaranteed to
make you look as cute as a button,
however you wear it.

Everything you will need...

Leather scraps can be picked up from fabric and craft shops at bargain prices and used to create any number of sweet or spectacular brooch projects.

1 Leather scraps in three different colours

2 1in (25mm) pin back

Craft glue

Hole punch

Scissors

mickey

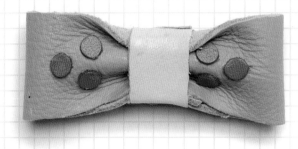

Assembling mickey

1 Cut out two leather strips in two different colours – one 6¼ x 1½in (160 x 40mm), the other ¾ x 3in (20 x 80mm).

2 Create a loop with the longer leather strip and glue the edges together. Hold the glued area firmly with your fingers until the glue dries.

3 Turn the piece over and pinch the front side between your thumb and index finger until it forms a neat bow shape.

4 Using your other hand, tightly wrap the shorter strip around the pinched area to secure it and hold tightly.

5 Turn over and thread the pin back through the smaller leather strip, so the underside faces the back of the larger strip, and glue into place.

6 Using a hole punch, make six circles (or more if you like) from the remaining leather scraps. Trim around the dots with nail scissors to remove any messy fibres.

7 Glue three dots onto each half of the bow and allow to dry.

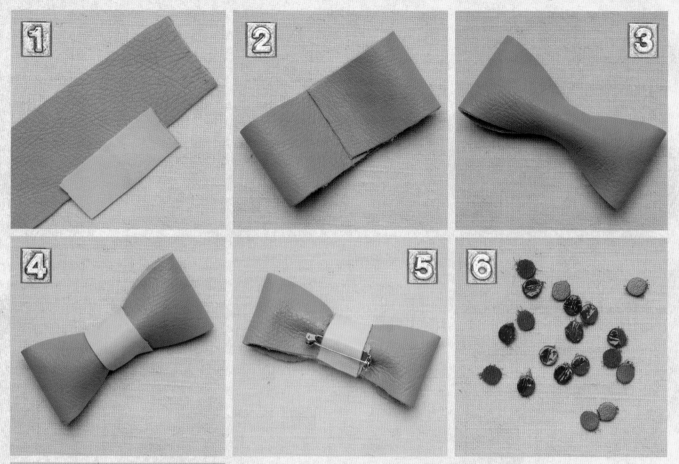

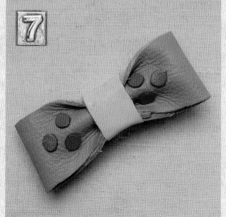

MIX AND MATCH THE COLOURED LEATHER
FOR A BROOCH TO GO WITH ANY OUTFIT.

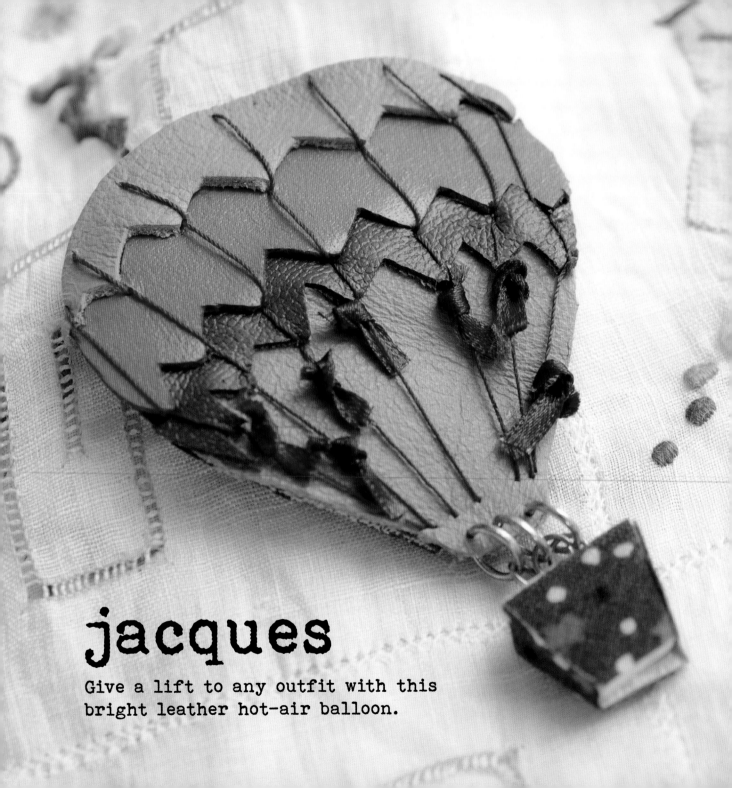

jacques

Give a lift to any outfit with this
bright leather hot-air balloon.

Everything you will need...

The movable basket gently swings with your every step –
making you feel as though you could simply float away.

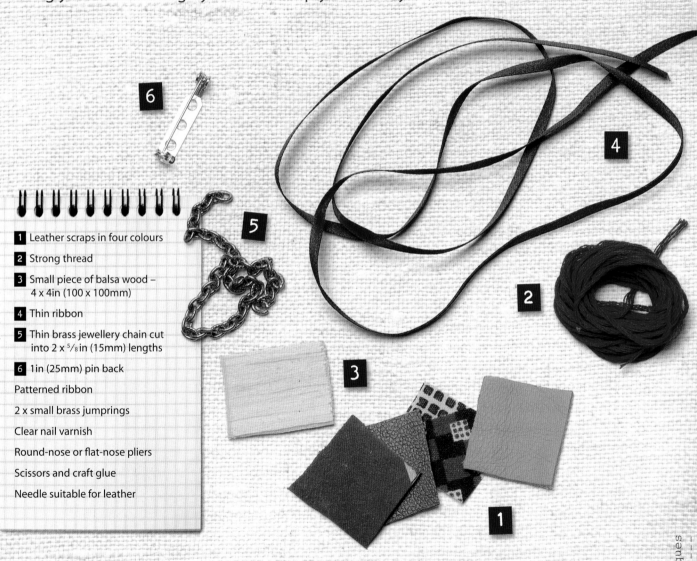

1. Leather scraps in four colours
2. Strong thread
3. Small piece of balsa wood –
   4 x 4in (100 x 100mm)
4. Thin ribbon
5. Thin brass jewellery chain cut
   into 2 x ⁵⁄₈ in (15mm) lengths
6. 1in (25mm) pin back

Patterned ribbon

2 x small brass jumprings

Clear nail varnish

Round-nose or flat-nose pliers

Scissors and craft glue

Needle suitable for leather

Assembling jacques

1 Cut out leather pieces using the balloon template.

2 Glue the smaller, decorative balloon elements into place on the larger balloon-shaped piece.

3 Sew from the triangle peaks of each piece to the peaks of the one below using a loose running stitch, finishing in a straight line at the base. Don't worry if the back looks messy; you will be covering it up later.

4 Loop lengths of the thin ribbon around the bottom row of stitches and tie into a series of tight double knots. Trim so that only $2/5$ in (10mm) hangs on either side of the stitch. Paint the ribbon ends with clear nail varnish to stop them fraying.

5 Use the template to cut out two 'baskets' from balsa wood. Cover one side of each piece with glue and lay face down on the 'wrong side' of patterned ribbon.

6 Leave the baskets to dry before trimming around the edges to remove excess ribbon. Glue the other sides of basket pieces and sandwich both $5/8$ in (15mm) lengths of chain between them. Make sure the chains are parallel with $1/5$ in (5mm) exposed at the top.

7 Make two small holes at the base of the balloon $1/5$ in (5mm) apart. Use pliers to open the jumprings (see page 26) before looping them through. Thread the exposed ends of the chain through the jumprings and snap them closed with pliers.

8 Glue the final leather piece to the balloon back and secure the pin back.

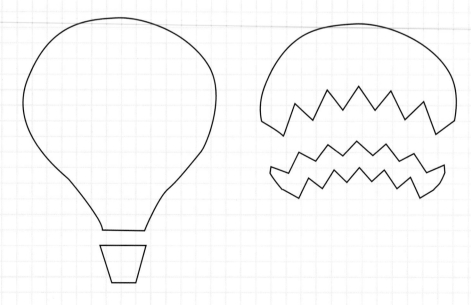

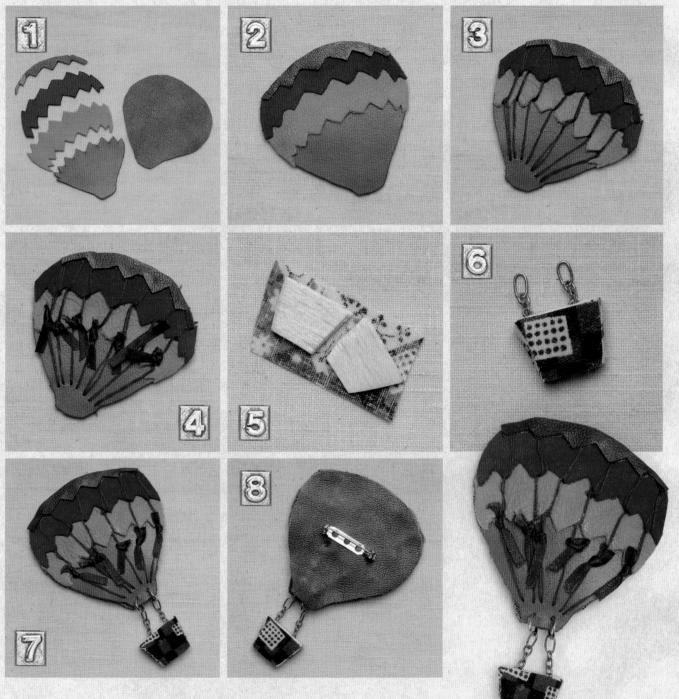

ribbons
and buttons

lee

Reward – and decorate
– a talented friend
with their very own
military-style medal.

Everything you will need...

Use a treble clef for a music virtuoso, an owl for a brainiac or – for an all-rounder – you might need to create a whole set!

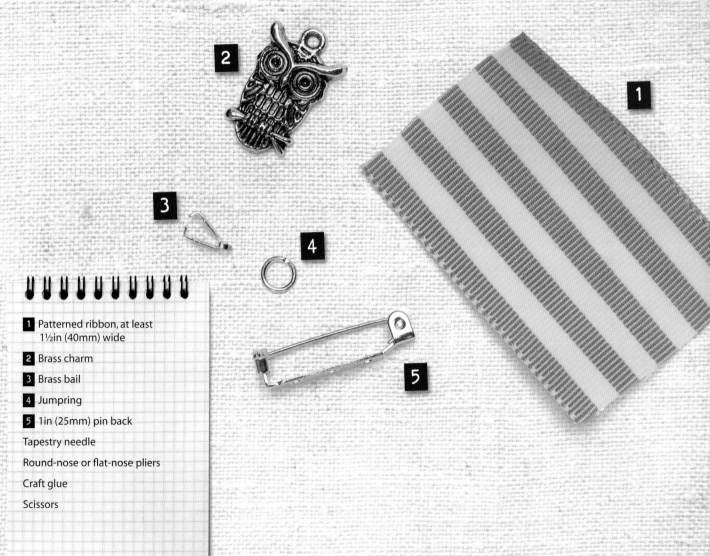

1 Patterned ribbon, at least 1½in (40mm) wide

2 Brass charm

3 Brass bail

4 Jumpring

5 1in (25mm) pin back

Tapestry needle

Round-nose or flat-nose pliers

Craft glue

Scissors

Assembling lee

1 Cut a 3½ in (90mm) length of ribbon. Fold in half vertically and run your fingernail along the edge a few times to make a strong line. Apply a thin layer of craft glue between the two halves and leave it to dry.

2 Trim both corners off one end of the ribbon to form a point, then cut the tip off.

3 Use the tapestry needle to make a small hole in the end you have just trimmed. It should be centred and about ⅛ in (5mm) from the edge.

4 Thread the brass bail through the hole and squeeze the pins of your bail together to close.

5 Open the jumpring, loop it through the charm, before snapping it closed over the bail.

6 Your charm should be positioned neatly and facing upwards.

7 Turn the ribbon over and thread the other end through a pin back.

8 Fold the ribbon over the pin back and secure into place with a thin layer of craft glue – you might need to hold this in place with your finger until it dries.

STOP THE RIBBON
FROM FRAYING BY
APPLYING A THIN
COAT OF CLEAR
NAIL VARNISH
TO THE EDGES.

lee

tatty

With just a little imagination, a tape measure can be transformed into a gorgeous rosette.

Everything you will need...

This project is quick and easy to make, and perfect
for the novice craft maker as well as the more skilled.

1 Brightly coloured tape measure

2 Strong thread to match tape
measure

3 Quirky button

4 1in (25mm) brooch back

Leather needle

Craft glue

Scissors

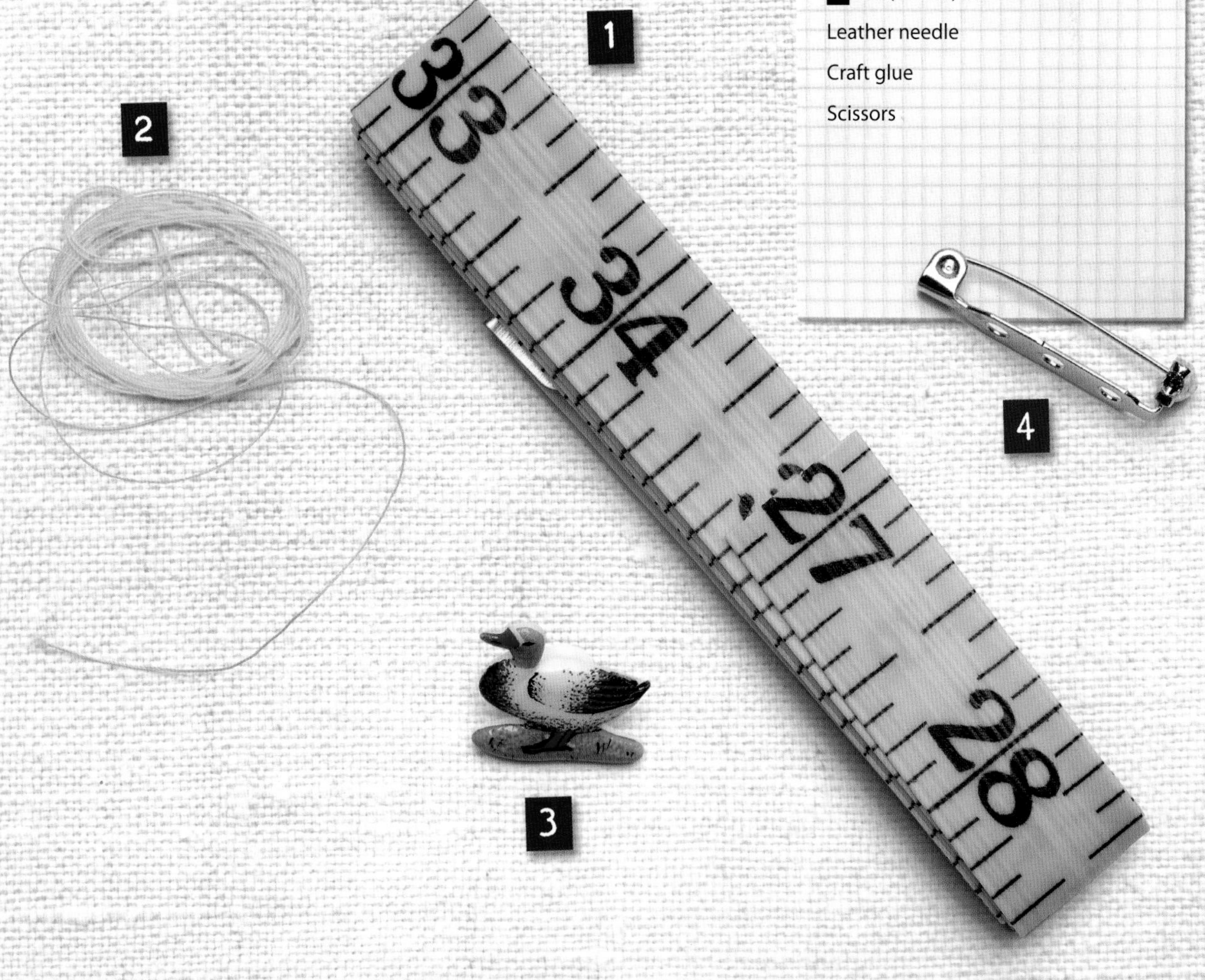

1

2

3

4

tatty

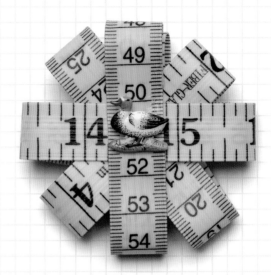

Assembling tatty

1 Take one end of your tape measure and make a loop 2½in (63mm) long.

2 Pressing it down with your finger, sew the loop into place with two or three small stitches in the middle.

3 Fold over the remaining length of tape at a 45-degree angle.

4 Turn over and make another loop and press down with your finger and then sew into place with two or three small stitches.

5 Repeat steps 3 and 4 and stitch until you have eight loops. Trim off the remaining length of tape so you are left with about 1½in (40mm).

6 Thread this remaining tape through the pin back so that the pin side is facing out. Smear the flap with a thin layer of craft glue and fold the tape back over the brooch back.

7 Glue the button to the front side and hold in place with your finger until the glue dries.

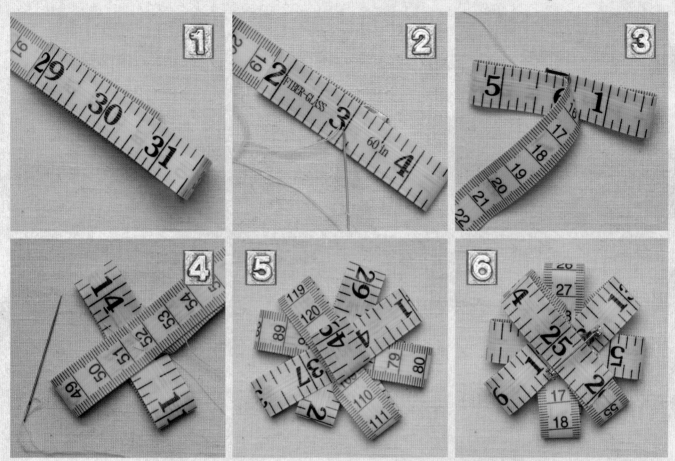

INSTEAD OF SEWING THIS BROOCH, YOU CAN JUST AS EASILY ASSEMBLE IT WITH CRAFT GLUE.

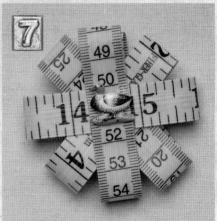

doris

Do something creative
with the doilies that
your grandma keeps
giving you.

Everything you will need...

Simply cut, sew and add a pretty button for a versatile corsage, or pin it to your favourite cardigan or onto a loop of elastic for a chic headband.

x2

1 2 x vintage cotton doilies in different colours

2 Thread to match both doilies

3 2 x felt squares to match one of the doilies, measuring 3 x 3in (80 x 80mm)

4 1 x pretty button

1in (25mm) pin back

Pins

Needle

Scissors

Craft glue

doris

Assembling doris

1 Cut out a semicircular piece from one of your doilies, making sure it is at least 8in (200mm) wide.

2 Pin the ends together so the border forms a circle and secure with a pin. Then cut a smaller circle in the centre and trim away any messy edges. We'll call this 'doily 1'.

3 Place doily 1 onto one of the felt squares – spreading it out to form a fairly even circle – and pin into place.

4 Repeat steps 1 and 2 with the second doily – which we'll call 'doily 2' – but make it slightly smaller than doily 1.

5 Place doily 2 onto doily 1 and pin into place.

6 Sew doily 1 onto the felt in running stitch, using matching thread. Next sew around the edge of doily 2 in running stitch with matching thread to attach it to doily 1.

7 Cut out a circle the same size as doily 1 from the remaining felt square (keep the scraps) and glue onto the back of the felt square. Then trim off the felt square so it is the same size as the circle you've just glued into place.

8 Place the pin back onto the middle of the felt circle. Cut a small square from the leftover felt scraps, slightly smaller than the width of your brooch back. Thread under the brooch pin and glue into place.

9 Finally, sew your pretty button into the centre of doily 2, making sure you don't sew deeper than the two doilies.

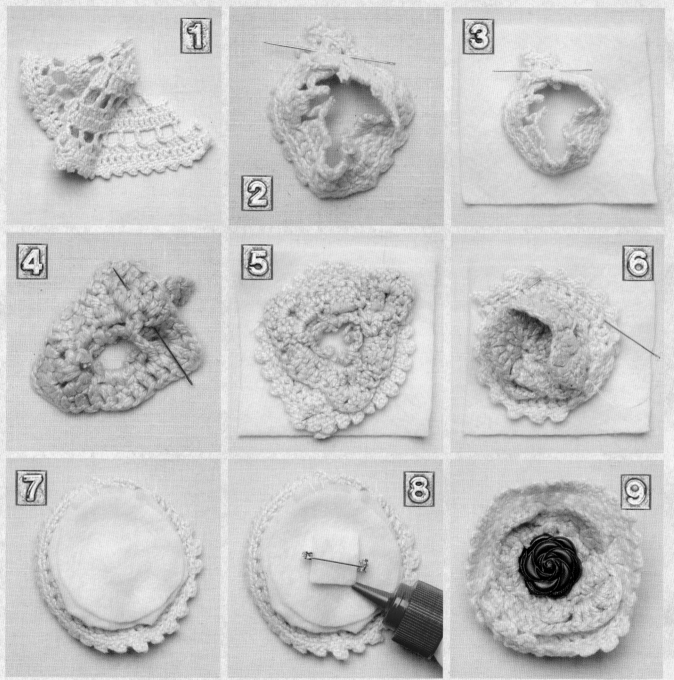

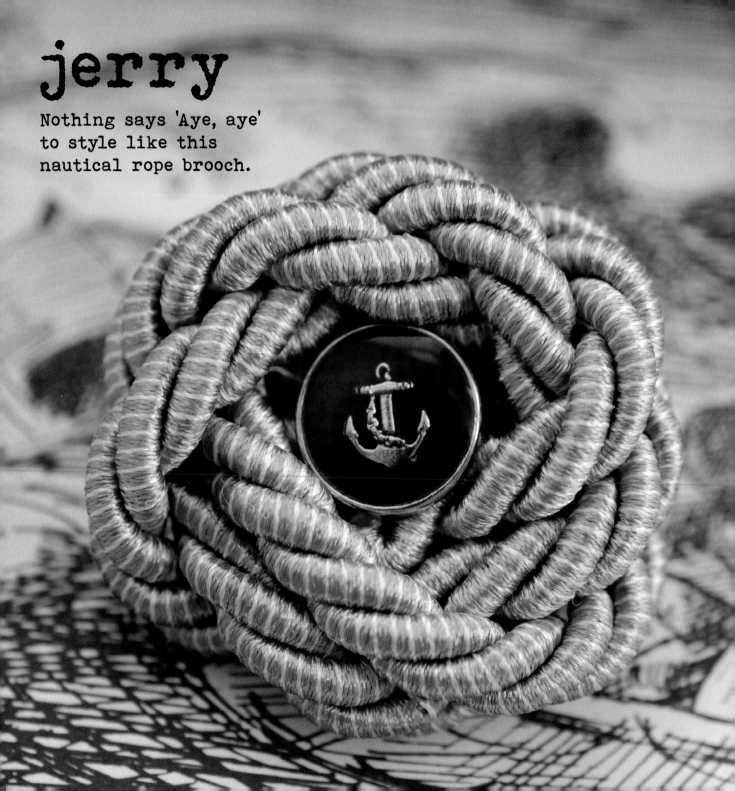

jerry

Nothing says 'Aye, aye'
to style like this
nautical rope brooch.

Everything you will need...

Practise this project with string or shoelaces a few times before moving onto thick gold or silver cord for a striking result.

1 25in (635mm) of thick gold cord

2 1 x blazer button

3 Scrap of felt

4 1in (25mm) pin back

Sticky tape

Craft glue

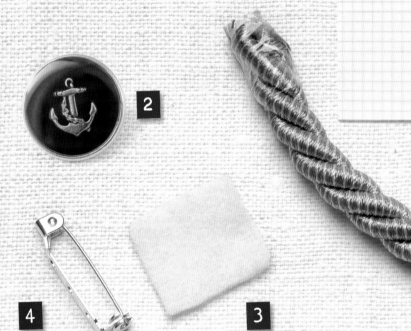

Assembling jerry

1 Secure both ends of the thick cord with sticky tape to prevent it from unravelling. Place the cord onto your work surface and cross the left end over the right making sure the two ends are an equal length from the crossing point.

2 Wind the left end halfway around the loop, then do the same with the right end until they are side-by-side again.

3 Hold your rope circle in one hand and, with the other hand, pull one end at a time to tighten everything up.

4 Wind the left end halfway around the loop (as you did in step 2), but this time weave in and out of the previous loop.

5 Repeat the process in step 4 with the right end. Tighten everything up.

6 Turn your rope circle over so you're looking at the 'wrong' side.

7 Tuck the left end into the centre of the circle and glue into place, then repeat the process with the right end.

8 Cut a small circle from your felt scrap, around 1½in (40mm) in diameter, and place over the two ends you have just glued into place. Add a brooch back and cover with a small square of felt. Glue into place.

9 Finally, turn over your rope circle so you're looking at the 'right' side and glue the nautical button into the centre. Leave to dry.

vintage
and found

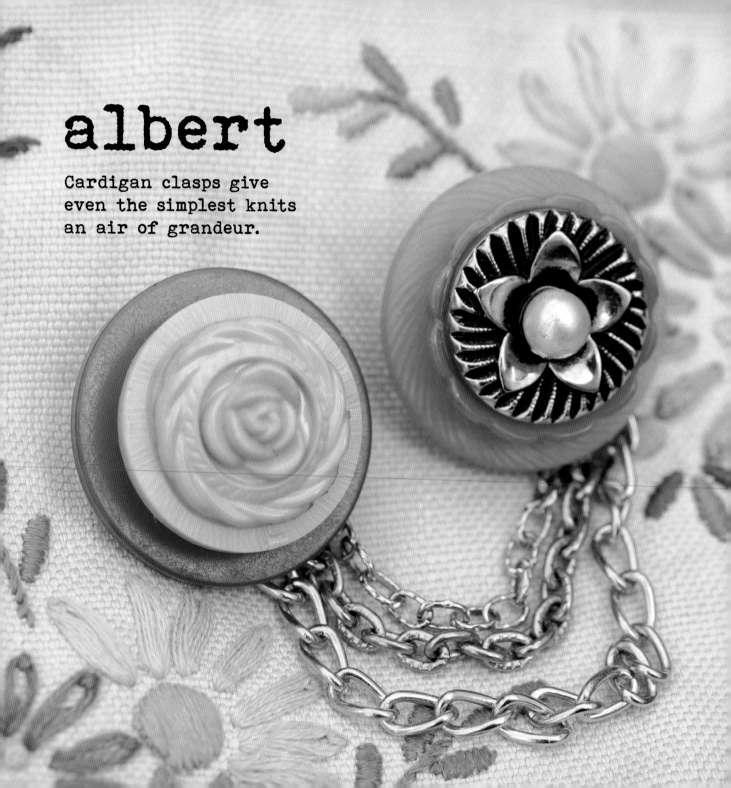

albert

Cardigan clasps give
even the simplest knits
an air of grandeur.

Everything you will need...

You can use any buttons and jewellery chains that tickle your fancy for this project. I combined Bakelite buttons with brass, gold and silver chains to create an eclectic, vintage look.

1 Selection of pretty buttons with flat surfaces in various sizes

2 Length of jewellery chain at least 18in (500mm) long

3 2 x pin backs smaller than your largest buttons

2 x brass jumprings

Craft glue

x2

Assembling albert

1 Choose six buttons of various sizes from a collection of vintage buttons.

2 Stack three buttons into ascending order (largest at the bottom, smallest on the top) and glue into place. Now make another stack and glue. Leave them to dry.

3 Glue a pin back to the underside of each button stack.

4 Cut your length of jewellery chain into three pieces: 1 x 5in (127mm), 1 x 6in (152mm) and 1 x 7in (178mm).

5 Thread one end of each chain length through a jumpring and snap the ring closed. Do the same for the other end.

6 Finally, open each pin back, thread through one end of the gathered chains and close.

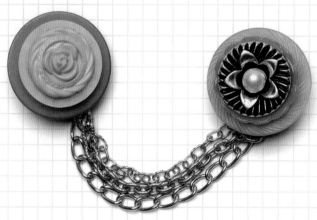

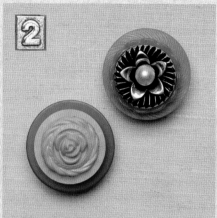

DON'T MAKE YOUR 'BUTTON STACKS' IDENTICAL.

IT'S THE MISMATCH THAT ADDS CHARM TO THIS PROJECT.

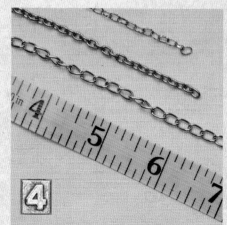

albert

james

This upcycling project is a clever way to transform old maps and crumpled street directories.

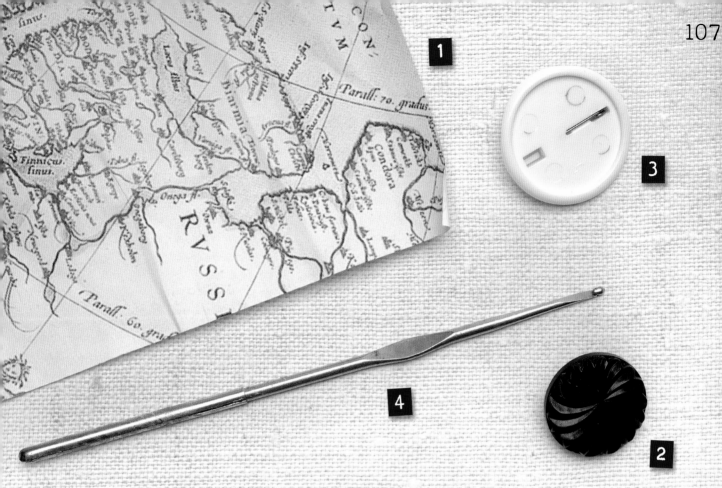

Everything you will need...

Old maps have an interesting colour palette for making beads, but you can just as easily use patterned paper such as giftwrap for a different effect.

1 Old map or giftwrap cut to around 12 x 8in (30 x 21cm) – keep any off-cuts

2 Pretty vintage button

3 1¹/₈in (30mm) button badge

4 Crochet hook or skewer

Wood glue – PVA or Mod Podge

Scalpel

Metal ruler

james

Assembling james

1 Mark 1$^1/_8$in (30mm) intervals along the length of your map at either end.

2 Use your scalpel and ruler to cut from the first 1$^1/_8$in (30mm) mark at one end to the 0 mark at the opposite end to form a long, skinny triangle. Then turn your map upside down and do the same again. Repeat until you have about 12 triangles.

3 Cut each skinny triangle piece horizontally to make two smaller triangles.

4 Take one triangle piece and place the wider base along your crochet hook or skewer. Wrap the base around the hook or skewer lightly and squeeze a line of glue onto the remaining length.

5 Continue to wrap the piece around – tightly, but making sure it can still slide off – moving up and down the hook or skewer to form a barrel-shaped bead.

6 Slide the barrel bead off the hook or skewer and use your fingers to smear with glue. Leave to dry. Repeat steps 3–4 until you have about 24 beads.

7 Glue scrap pieces of your paper over the front of the button badge.

8 While the glue is still wet on the button badge, arrange the beads around the circumference in two layers.

9 Finish by gluing a vintage button right into the centre.

PRACTISE WITH SCRAP PAPER UNTIL YOU FEEL CONFIDENT ENOUGH TO USE THE REAL THING.

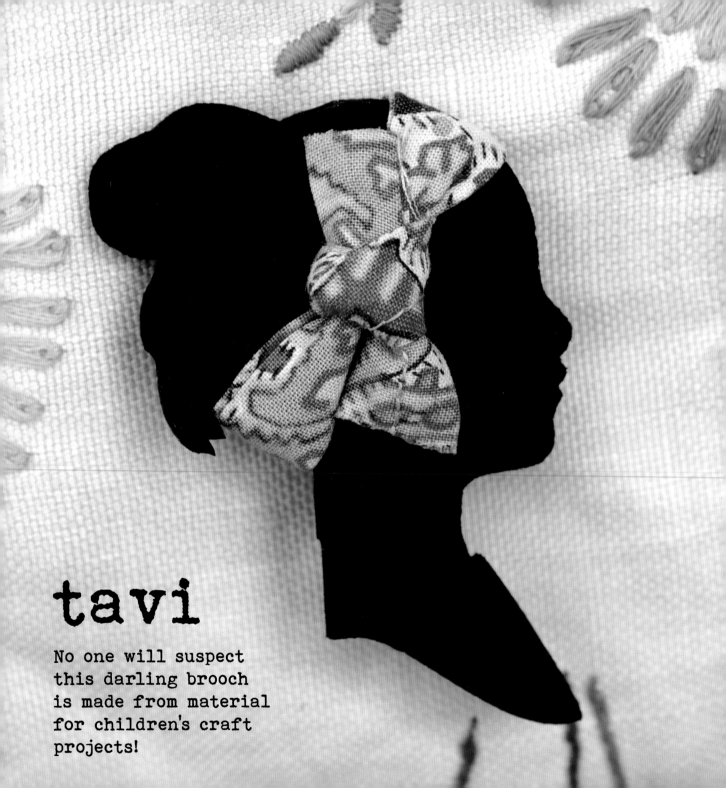

tavi

No one will suspect
this darling brooch
is made from material
for children's craft
projects!

Everything you will need...

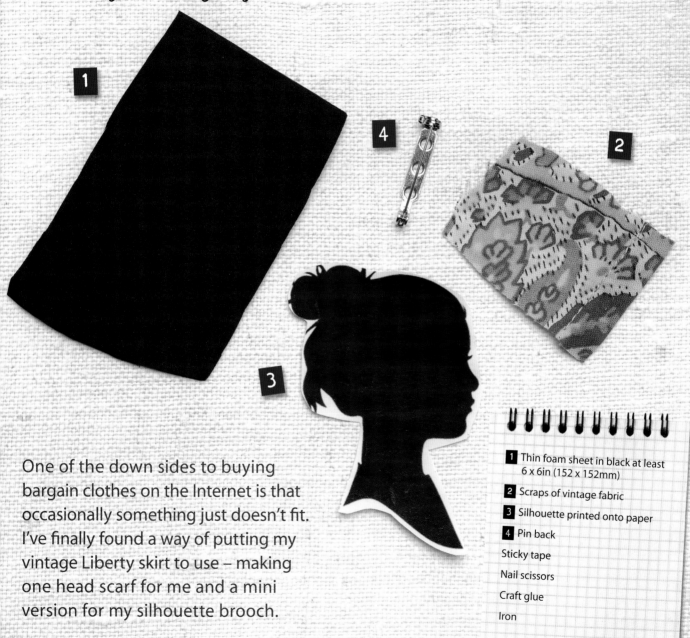

One of the down sides to buying bargain clothes on the Internet is that occasionally something just doesn't fit. I've finally found a way of putting my vintage Liberty skirt to use – making one head scarf for me and a mini version for my silhouette brooch.

1 Thin foam sheet in black at least 6 x 6in (152 x 152mm)

2 Scraps of vintage fabric

3 Silhouette printed onto paper

4 Pin back

Sticky tape

Nail scissors

Craft glue

Iron

tavi

Assembling tavi

1 Print out a silhouette shape and cut around it, leaving a thin white border.

2 Attach the shape to the foam sheet with sticky tape.

3 Carefully cut around the edge of the silhouette using nail scissors.

4 Repeat the first three steps, so you have two identical foam silhouettes. Glue these together and leave to dry.

5 Cut your vintage fabric into a 12 x 1in (300 x 25mm) strip, fold horizontally into three and iron into shape.

6 Wrap the fabric strip around the silhouette's head, tie in a knot or bow and trim off any excess fabric.

7 Turn the silhouette over. Open the pin back, slide the metal bar under the fabric, swing the pin over and close. Secure with a dab of glue.

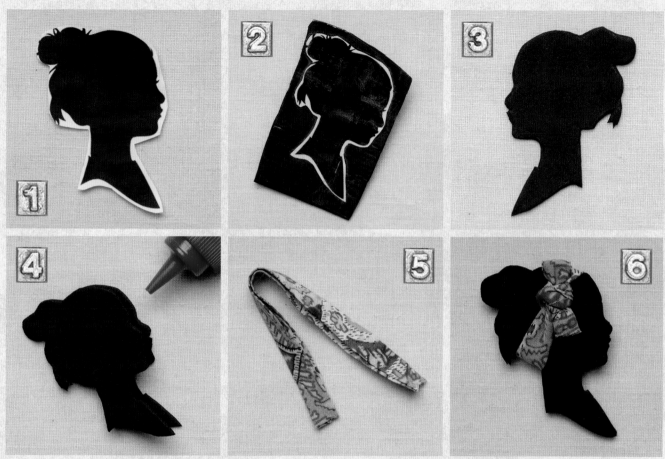

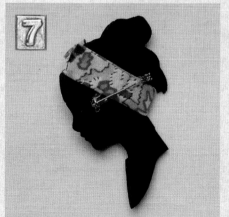

YOU CAN FIND FOAM SHEETS IN MOST CRAFT STORES, AND THEY ARE DIRT CHEAP!

dom

The edges of these vintage
botanical prints were a bit
shabby, so I didn't feel too
guilty about cutting them up.

Everything you will need...

Domino tiles are fantastic bases for altered art
and the perfect shape for making brooches.
The possibilities are endless.

1 Vintage domino

2 Lovely patterned paper

3 1in (25mm) pin back

Wood glue – PVA or Mod Podge

Varnish or clear resin

Craft glue

Nail scissors

Assembling dom

1 Place the domino onto your paper and trace around the edges. Use nail scissors to cut the paper to shape.

2 Smear wood glue onto the domino using a paintbrush or your finger.

3 Top the domino with the paper piece and smooth down.

4 Apply more glue to the paper and smear over the surface using either a paintbrush or your finger.

5 Mix a two-part clear resin (see pages 16-17). When the paper is dry, apply a layer of clear resin (or high-gloss varnish) onto the surface of the paper using a stick. Leave to dry – you'll need to allow 12–14 hours if you're using resin.

6 Finally, glue the pin back to the back.

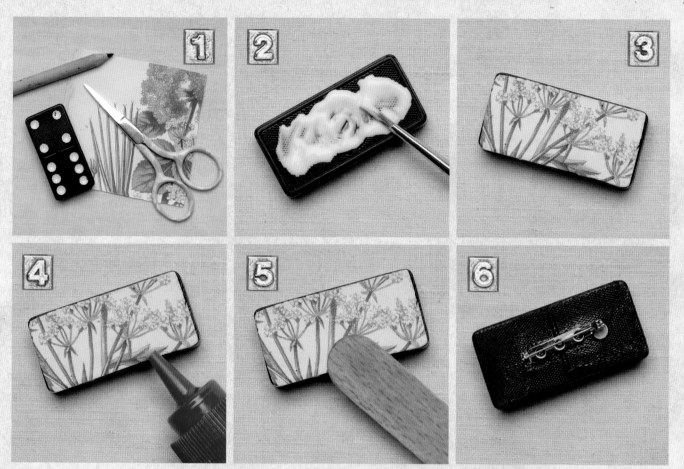

WOODEN DOMINO TILES MAKE THE BEST BASE
BUT ARE QUITE HARD TO FIND. TRY THRIFT
STORES OR INTERNET AUCTION SITES.

resources

BOOKS

Fabulous Jewelry from Found Objects: Creative Projects, Simple Techniques by Marthe Le Van (Sterling, 2007)

Meet me at Mike's: 26 Fun and Crafty Projects by Pip Lincolne (Hardie Grant, 2009)

Non-precious Jewellery: Methods and Techniques by Kathie Murphy (A&C Black, 2009)

The Art of Resin Jewelry: Techniques and Projects for Creating Stylish Designs by Sherri Haab (Watson-Guptill, 2006)

WEBSITES

Cut Out and Keep
www.cutoutandkeep.net

Design Sponge
www.designspongeonline.com

Instructables
www.instructables.com

Readymade
www.readymade.com

SOURCES OF MATERIALS

UK

Artifolk
Kear Limited
Unit G4
Railway Triangle
Portsmouth
Hampshire
PO6 1TQ
www.artifolk.co.uk

Beads Unlimited
The Brighton Bead Shop
21 Sydney Street
Brighton
BN1 4EN
www.beadsunlimited.co.uk

Fred Aldous
37 Lever Street
Manchester
M1 1LW
www.fredaldous.co.uk
sales@fredaldous.net
Tel: +44 (0)161 236 4224

Just Beads
Unit 10, Clock House Farm
Lea Road
Lea Preston
PR4 0RA
sales@justbeads.co.uk
Tel: +44(0)1772 978 029

Misi
www.misi.co.uk

Sparkles
www.sparklesgroup.co.uk

USA

Bocage
PO BOX 5662
Santa Barbara, California
93150-5662
www.bocagenewyork.com
info@bocagenewyork.com

Sacred Kitsch Studio
P.O. Box 5000
Chico, California 95927
info@sacredkitschstudio.com
www.sacredkitschstudio.com

S.Axelrod Co.
70 West Street
New York NY 10001
www.axelrodco.com
Tel: +1 212 594 3022

Sky Blue Pink
www.skybluepink.com

AUSTRALIA

Beads on Kelly Street
www.boks.com.au

Beads online
PO Box 160
Tweed Heads
New South Wales
Australia 2485
sales@beadsonline.com.au
www.beadsonline.com.au

Benjamin's Crafts
868 Beaufort Street
Inglewood
Western Australia 6052
www.benjaminscrafts.com.au

Eckersleys
www.eckersleys.com.au

Over the Rainbow
PO Box 9112 Seaford
Victoria, Australia 3198
Tel: +61 (0)3 9785 3800
www.polymerclay.com.au

GENERAL

For jewellery supplies and inspiration

Etsy
www.etsy.com

Empire Beads
www.empirebeads.co.uk
www.empirebeads.com.au

about the author

Louise Compagnone has worked as an editor and writer for nearly 10 years, covering topics from food and travel to fashion and music. Her work has been published on the web and in a number of international publications including *The Australian* newspaper.

Growing up in a tiny town in Western Australia, Louise learnt to make everything from patchwork quilts and macramé owls to her grandma's tomato sauce and, most importantly, her own fun. Her quirky handmade jewellery combines new, vintage and found materials, and has been sold in boutiques around the world.

She currently lives in Brighton, UK with her partner and their weird hairless cat (who loves to run off with laboured-over craft items in his mouth).

index

Project names are given in italics

To place an order, or to request
a catalogue, contact:

GMC Publications Ltd
Castle Place,
166 High Street,
Lewes,
East Sussex,
BN7 1XU
United Kingdom

Tel: +44 (0)1273 488005
Fax: +44 (0)1273 402866

www.gmcbooks.com